HORSEPOWER

DRAGSTERS

by Matt Doeden

Reading Consultant:
Barbara J. Fox
Reading Specialist
North Carolina State University

Capstone
press

Mankato, Minnesota

Blazers is published by Capstone Press
151 Good Counsel Drive, P.O. Box 669, Mankato, Minnesota 56002
www.capstonepress.com

Library of Congress Cataloging-in-Publication Data
Doeden, Matt.
    Dragsters / by Matt Doeden.
    p. cm.—(Blazers. horsepower)
    Includes bibliographical references and index.
    ISBN 0-7368-2735-8 (hardcover)
    1. Drag racing—Juvenile literature. 2. Dragsters—Juvenile
literature.
I. Title. II. Series: Blazers. horsepower.
GV1029.3.D64 2005
796.72—dc22   2004003150

Summary: Discusses top fuel dragsters, their main features, and how
    they are raced.

Editorial Credits
Tom Adamson, editor; Jason Knudson, designer; Jo Miller, photo
    researcher; Eric Kudalis, product planning editor

Photo Credits
Artemis Images/Curtis Pilgreen, 11, 19
Auto Imagery Inc., 5, 6–7, 8–9, 12, 13, 17, 20–21, 23, 26
Getty Images/Jamie Squire, 23 (inset); Jon Ferrey, 15, 28–29;
    Mike Powell, cover
Mark Bruederle, 18
Mercury Press/Isaac Hernandez, 25
Racers Edge Photography, 14

1 2 3 4 5 6 09 08 07 06 05 04

The dragster roars down the drag strip. It crosses the finish line at more than 300 miles (480 kilometers) per hour.

A parachute opens behind the
dragster. The parachute helps slow
down the car. The race is over in less
than five seconds.

BLAZER FACT

Other types of dragsters
are funny cars and
pro stock dragsters.

DRAGSTER DESIGN

Top fuel dragsters are the fastest cars in the world. They are long, narrow, and lightweight.

Dragsters have loud, powerful hemi engines. Flames shoot out of the engine at the start of the race.

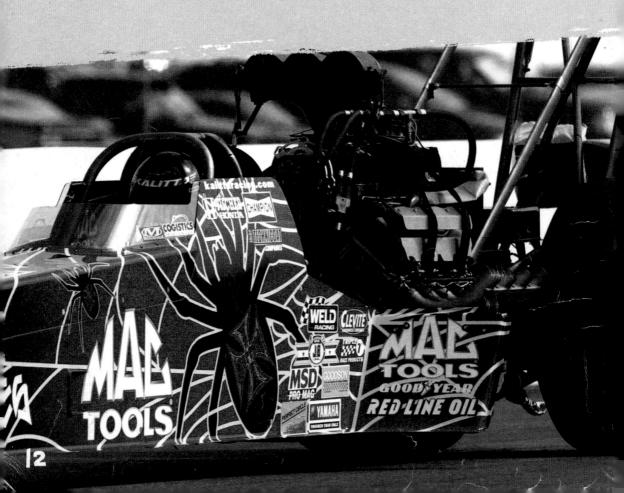

BLAZER FACT

Dragsters burn a whole tank of fuel in less than five seconds.

Crashes can happen. Bars
protect the drivers. Drivers wear a
helmet and gloves. They wear
fireproof clothing.

GRIPPING THE TRACK

Top fuel dragsters have a large wing. The wing helps the driver control the car.

Wing

Dragsters have large, wide rear tires called slicks. The slicks grip the drag strip. Slicks help the cars speed up quickly.

BLAZER FACT

A dragster's rear tires get wrinkles from the quick start.

DRAGSTER DIAGRAM

Driver

Drag strip

Wing

Engine

Slicks

DRAGSTERS IN ACTION

Two dragsters line up side by side with the engines running. A row of lights called a Christmas tree counts down to the start.

Christmas tree

23

The drivers stomp on their gas pedals. Every second counts. They speed up quickly but carefully. They don't want to lose control.

BLAZER FACT

Top fuel dragsters cost more than $100,000 to build.

Doug Kalitta

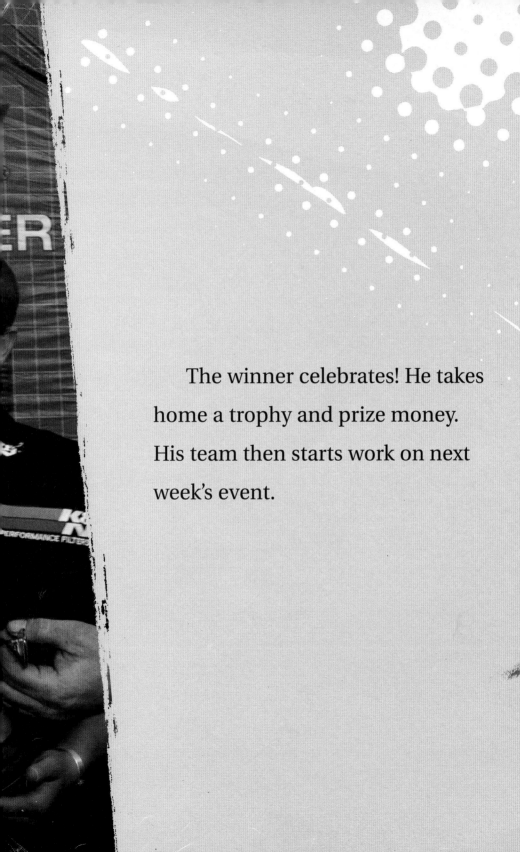

The winner celebrates! He takes home a trophy and prize money. His team then starts work on next week's event.

GLOSSARY

Christmas tree (KRISS-muhss TREE)—the row of lights that count off the seconds to start the race

drag strip (DRAG STRIP)—the track where dragsters race; drag strips are usually .25 mile (.4 kilometer) long.

hemi (HEM-ee)—an engine that burns fuel in chambers shaped like a ball cut in half; hemi is short for hemisphere.

parachute (PAIR-uh-shoot)—a large piece of strong fabric that flies out behind a dragster at the end of the race; the parachute helps slow down the car.

slicks (SLIKS)—soft tires that have no tread

wing (WING)—the part attached to the back of a dragster designed to help the rear tires grip the track

READ MORE

Bledsoe, Glen, and Karen Bledsoe. *The World's Fastest Dragsters.* Built for Speed. Mankato, Minn.: Capstone Press, 2003.

Deady, Kathleen W. *Dragsters.* Wild Rides! Mankato, Minn.: Capstone Press, 2002.

Pitt, Matthew. *Drag Racer.* Built for Speed. New York: Children's Press, 2001.

INTERNET SITES

FactHound offers a safe, fun way to find Internet sites related to this book. All of the sites on FactHound have been researched by our staff.

Here's how:

1. Visit *www.facthound.com*
2. Type in this special code **0736827358** for age-appropriate sites. Or enter a search word related to this book for a more general search.
3. Click on the **Fetch It** button.

FactHound will fetch the best sites for you!

INDEX